Why Am I Conservative?

Melanie Elliott

Why Am I Conservative?

Melanie Angell Elliott

24 topics for kids or anyone

Tate Publishing & Enterprises

Published by Tate Publishing & Enterprises, LLC
127 E. Trade Center Terrace | Mustang, Oklahoma 73064 USA
1.888.361.9473 | www.tatepublishing.com

Tate Publishing is committed to excellence in the publishing industry. The company reflects the philosophy established by the founders, based on Psalm 68:11,
"The Lord gave the word and great was the company of those who published it."

Published in the United States of America

ISBN: 978-1-61663-437-7
1. Political Science: Political Ideologies: Conservatism and Liberalism
2. Political Science: General
10.05.12

Table of Contents

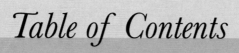

Foreword

by Bryan Fischer

As Ronald Reagan observed, "Freedom is never more than one generation away from extinction. We didn't pass it to our children in the bloodstream. It must be fought for, protected, and handed on for them to do the same."

With an out-of-control federal judiciary robbing us of more constitutional liberties and freedoms virtually every day, and power-hungry congressional leaders imposing more regulations and higher taxes on American citizens every day, it is imperative that we make a fresh effort to impart to the generation that will follow us a true understanding of the principles of liberty and the genius of the American experiment.

We once were able to count on our public system of education to teach fundamental American precepts such as religious liberty, limited government, personal freedom, personal responsibility and self-reliance. But no more. With non-conservative organizations such as the National Education Association imposing a social agenda on our students that our Founders would never recognize, the classroom has become more of an enemy than an ally in passing the torch of liberty to the next generation.

So we must turn, as we have so many times in the past, to America's parents to instill in their own children the sacred truths and principles that have made America the greatest nation in the history of the world.

Melanie Angell Elliott's book, *Why Am I Conservative?*, may be just the tool you need to do that with your own children.

Each bite-sized chapter crystallizes an important principle of American history and culture, and is augmented with quotes from Founding Fathers, the

✹ ✹ ✹

Bible and experts that alone are worth the price of the book.

Get this book, buy extra copies to give away, and whatever else you do, read it to your own children. They will thank you, and the next generation of Americans will thank you.

—Bryan Fischer
Director of Issues Analysis,
American Family Association
Host of the "Focal Point" radio program on
the American Family Radio Talk Network

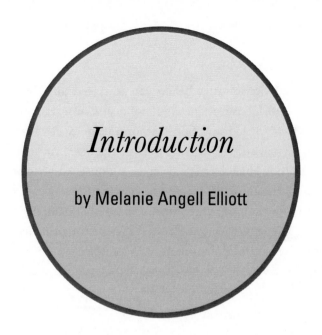

Introduction

by Melanie Angell Elliott

Dear Reader,

I am a Conservative parent raising two children. I am honored to teach them my values and beliefs, hoping they will adopt those beliefs as they grow. This book should help you educate your child or yourself about Conservatism and why it is a sensible choice over any other political worldview.

Some of my Conservative beliefs can be traced directly to the Bible. As a Conservative Christian, I believe the Bible's author (God) means what He says and the meaning does not change over time. Some

✸ ✸ ✸   11

of my Conservative beliefs can be traced directly to the US Constitution. As a political Conservative, I believe the Constitution's authors meant exactly what they said and its meaning does not change over time. An individual doesn't have to be a Conservative to be a Christian or a Christian to be a Conservative. But for me, the two belief systems fit together naturally.

Conservatism consists of belief in the principles on which the United States was founded:

- Freedom for individuals
- Free-market capitalism
- Private property rights
- Limited government

In this book I defend the established traditions that have caused the United States to prosper so bountifully.

I am proud to label myself a Conservative, but hesitate to label the opposite belief with any one particular term. Through history, individuals that are not Conservative have often been called bureaucrats, liberals, leftists, collectivists, socialists, statists, and progres-

✸ ✸ ✸

sives. In this book I will use the term "Nonconservative." Their beliefs are opposite of Conservatism:

- Individuals are not capable of managing their freedoms.

- Capitalism is bad because it causes unequal results.

- Property should be shared equally; no one deserves to have more than another.

- Government should have unlimited power and the ability to control the lives of citizens.

There are different degrees and fervency of being Conservative. If we disagree on a particular topic, I hope you will be motivated to think about it and research it. Maybe you'll change your mind, maybe not. Either way, your knowledge and strength of your beliefs will have increased, which is a good thing.

Because I wrote this book to be shared with young people, I kept the topics short and simple. Every topic can be explored in greater depth if you have the time and desire. To begin, try reading and talking about just one topic a day, and see where the conversation goes.

Children should be educated and instructed in the principles of freedom.

—John Adams

There is but one straight course, and that is to seek truth and pursue it steadily.

—George Washington

Train a child in the way he should go, and when he is old he will not turn from it.

Proverbs 22:6

✸ ✸ ✸

Love of Country

I am Conservative because I love my country.

The United States of America is the best country in the world. At its founding, our government was set up to allow maximum freedom for individuals: freedom to express ideas, pursue endeavors, and fulfill our purpose in life the way each one of us decides is best. America was founded with the promise of equality to each individual. When you call yourself a citizen of the United States, you can joyously embrace these ideals and proudly offer your national loyalty to the United States and your fellow citizens.

Nonconservatives in the United States tend to see themselves as citizens of the world first, and citizens of the United States second. Some want the United States to please foreign governments around the world instead of doing what is best for our own citizens. Some blame the United States for problems in the world. They focus on past mistakes the government has made, and its present shortcomings.

Conservatives and Nonconservatives agree that the United States is not a perfect place. However, we have different ideas for solving the problems. By following Conservative ideals, many of which you will find in this book, the United States will remain a great nation.

> The name of American, which belongs to you, in your national capacity, must always exalt the just pride of patriotism, more than any appellation derived from local discriminations.
> —George Washington

> The man who loves other countries as much as his own stands on a level with the man who loves other women as much as he loves his own wife.
> —Theodore Roosevelt

> God bless America, land that I love.
> —Irving Berlin

Dinner-Table Dialogue

- Is a country a better place when its citizens feel loyalty or love for it?

- How do you or others demonstrate loyalty and love for the United States?

- How is it possible to love someone or something imperfect (like a person or a country)?

- What can you do to help solve our country's problems?

✴ ✴ ✴   17

Belief in God

I am Conservative because I believe in the God of the Bible. God gave all humans the rights to life and liberty.

The United States Declaration of Independence supports the idea of God-given rights because it says all people are "…endowed by their Creator with certain unalienable Rights, that among these are Life, Liberty and the pursuit of Happiness." Good governments will recognize that some freedoms are granted by God alone. Our elected representatives (the people we choose to make decisions for us in the government) should not allow laws to take life or freedom away from innocent citizens.

Nonconservatives believe rights are given to people by the government. As a result, they believe elected representatives are allowed to make laws that take rights away.

There is a difference between God-given and government-given rights. Another way to describe them is freedoms (given by God) and privileges (granted by government). Freedoms should never be taken from innocent people. Privileges are granted to those who meet certain requirements like citizenship, age, and behavior.

> Kings or parliaments could not give the rights essential to happiness—we claim them from a higher source—from the King of kings and the Lord of all the Earth. They are not annexed to us by parchments or seals. They are created in us by the decrees of Providence, which establish the laws of our nature. They are born with us; and cannot be taken from us by any human power.
> —John Dickinson

> And can the liberties of a nation be thought secure when we have removed their only firm basis, a conviction in the minds of the people that

✴ ✴ ✴

these liberties are the gift of God? That they are not to be violated but with his wrath? Indeed I tremble for my country when I reflect that God is just: that his justice cannot sleep for ever.

—Thomas Jefferson

I will walk about in freedom, for I have sought out your precepts.

Psalm 119:45

It is for freedom that Christ has set us free. Stand firm, then, and do not let yourselves be burdened again by a yoke of slavery.

Galatians 5:1

✹ ✹ ✹

Dinner-Table Dialogue:

- What freedoms does God give to all people?

- What privileges does government grant to citizens?

✱ ✱ ✱

Founded on Faith

I am Conservative because I believe the United States was founded on faith in God.

Our country's founders recognized the hand of God in the creation of the United States. In spite of their different religious beliefs, they knew that God's blessings are the basis of our survival as a nation. Our founders wanted citizens to be free to choose their own faith and beliefs instead of being forced to follow an official government religion. Many references to God and faith are on important documents, monuments, and memorials in our nation's capital. Others are present in traditions and procedures. Citizens can choose to believe in God or not, but these references should not be removed.

Nonconservatives want to remove and forget our country's historical dependence on God. It seems they want to eliminate all references of historical faith from American public life, traditions and buildings. On the other hand, they tend to acknowledge and accommodate any religious faith except Christianity.

> The longer I live, the more convincing proofs I see of this truth—that God governs the affairs of men.
>
> —Benjamin Franklin

> It is the duty of all nations to acknowledge the Providence of Almighty God, to obey His will, to be grateful for His benefits, and humbly to implore His protection and favor.
>
> —George Washington

> No people can be bound to acknowledge and adore the invisible hand which conducts the affairs of men more than the people of the United States. Every step, by which they have advanced to the character of an independent

nation, seems to have been distinguished by some token of providential agency.

—George Washington

Almost all nations have peace or war at the will and pleasure of rulers whom they do not elect, and who are not always wise or virtuous. Providence has given to our people the choice of their rulers, and it is the duty as well as the privilege and interest of our Christian nation to select and prefer Christians for their rulers.

—John Jay

Dinner-Table Dialogue:

Info Quest:

- Does a citizen have to believe in God in order to be loyal and patriotic?

- What references to faith and God appear on documents, monuments, and memorials, or in the traditions and procedures of government?

- What efforts have been made to remove these references to faith and God?

US Constitution

I am Conservative because I believe the United States Constitution is the law our nation should follow.

The writers of the Constitution were very wise and experienced with government. Many thought government was a necessary evil; it was needed in order to have a stable society even though bad things happen to citizens when government becomes too powerful. The writers knew that when government allows citizens to live in freedom, happiness and prosperity will result. They did their best to write the Constitution so the federal (national) government would be limited, providing maximum freedom to states and individual citizens.

Every law that is passed for the country, any state, and any city must agree with the Constitution. When a law is thought to be unconstitutional, a judge or group of judges must interpret it by comparing it to the Constitution.

Conservatives trust the wisdom and experience of the Constitution's writers. They want to preserve and follow the original meaning of the Constitution because it provides timeless rules and boundaries to guide us. It is a legal document that outlines limits on government for citizens' protection. However, it can be changed through the amendment process outlined in the Constitution itself.

Nonconservatives want the meaning of the Constitution to shift as time passes and society changes. They tend to view the Constitution according to their personal opinions, life experiences, and the evolving standards of society. In this view, there are no limits to the power of government and citizens are not protected from it.

✷ ✷ ✷

On every question of construction (of the Constitution) let us carry ourselves back to the time when the Constitution was adopted, recollect the spirit manifested in the debates, and instead of trying what meaning may be squeezed out of the text, or invented against it, conform to the probable one in which it was passed.

—Thomas Jefferson

The Constitution means what it says. You figure out what it was understood to mean when it was adopted and that's the end of it. If you want more rights, create them by statute; if you want more constitutional rights, create them by amending the Constitution.

—Supreme Court Justice Antonin Scalia

Dinner-Table Dialogue:

- Which is the better way to change the Constitution: amend it through the process outlined in the Constitution, or allow a few judges to decide?

- Does good advice stay valid, even though times change? Give some examples of old but good advice.

Info Quest:

- What are the steps to amend the Constitution?

Virtue and Moral Behavior

I am Conservative because I believe in virtue, moral behavior, and a standard of right and wrong.

Citizens should live up to a standard of behavior that includes honesty, courtesy, generosity, and obedience to the rule of law. This behavior leads to peace and a satisfying life. As a result, an entire society becomes stable and prosperous.

Conservatives and Nonconservatives probably agree on this. Unfortunately, Nonconservatives tend to believe that individuals, not God, decide what is right and wrong. This is called moral relativism, and it makes it impossible to agree on one standard of right or wrong. Without belief in God, it is difficult to understand how or why to make moral choices.

> The propitious smiles of Heaven can never be expected on a nation that disregards the eternal rules of order and right, which Heaven itself has ordained.
>
> —George Washington

> Religion and good morals are the only solid foundation of public liberty and happiness.
>
> —Samuel Adams

> We have no government armed with power capable of contending with human passions unbridled by morality and religion. Avarice, ambition, revenge, or gallantry, would break the strongest cords of our Constitution as a whale goes through a net. Our Constitution was made only for a moral and religious people. It is wholly inadequate to the government of any other.
>
> —John Adams

> He has showed you, O man, what is good. And what does the Lord require of you? To

✹ ✹ ✹

act justly and to love mercy and to walk humbly with your God.

Micah 6:8

But the fruit of the Spirit is love, joy, peace, patience, kindness, goodness, faithfulness, gentleness and self-control. Against such things there is no law.

Galatians 5:22–23

Dinner-Table Dialogue:

- Who gets to decide right from wrong for all people at all times?

- What would happen if each individual got to decide for themselves what laws or rules to abide by? How would this affect crime, traffic, definitions of words, or playing games?

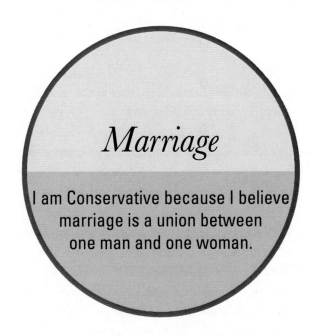

Marriage

I am Conservative because I believe marriage is a union between one man and one woman.

Conservatives believe lifelong marriage between one man and one woman is a very important part of a successful society. This is called traditional marriage or natural marriage. Men and women who marry are both usually better off as a result. Natural marriage causes adults to focus their energy toward honest work in order to build a life together and provide for any children who may bless their home. In this way, natural marriage protects the well-being of children. Strong, intact families tend to provide for each other, stabilize society, work toward the common good, and produce virtuous citizens.

When families break down, they are more likely to experience poverty, disorder, and crime. Government then gets involved in a number of ways, including welfare, child-support enforcement, court-managed family life, and police interaction. Without stable families, personal liberty for everyone is endangered because the laws to deal with these problems affect everyone.

Conservatives want more liberty and less government intrusion into citizens' lives. This is why many oppose efforts by government and certain groups to change the definition of marriage to include unions of two men, two women, or just about anything else anyone might think of. Marriage is too important to experiment with. Expanding marriage to every definition weakens the bonds of commitment, through all society, which keep a family together. Expanding marriage to include anyone ignores centuries of historical evidence that every child needs a mother and father. Whatever is best for children is, in the end, best for the United States because children are our future leaders.

> There is certainly no country in the world where the tie of marriage is more respected than in America, or where [wedded] happi-

✹ ✹ ✹

ness is more highly or worthily appreciated. In Europe almost all the disturbances of society arise from the irregularities of domestic life. To despise the natural bonds and legitimate pleasure of home is to contract a taste for excesses, a restlessness of heart, and fluctuating desires.

—Alexis De Tocqueville

It is the man and woman united that make the complete human being…Together they are more likely to succeed in the world.

—Benjamin Franklin

The Lord God said, "It is not good for the man to be alone. I will make a helper suitable for him."…Then the Lord God made a woman from the rib he had taken out of the man, and he brought her to the man.

Genesis 2:18, 22

But at the beginning of creation God made them male and female. For this reason a man will leave his father and mother and be united to his wife, and the two will become one flesh. So they are no longer two, but one. Therefore what God has joined together, let man not separate.

Mark 10:6–9

✱ ✱ ✱

Dinner-Table Dialogue:

- Not everyone is allowed to get married. What are the legal requirements? (Think about age, sex, species, family relationship, number of people, current marital status ...) What is your opinion about these requirements?

- What are some solutions to the problem of divorce?

- Conservatives are usually in favor of more individual freedoms, but they value and defend established traditions. How do Conservatives justify limiting marriage to one man and one woman only?

✹ ✹ ✹

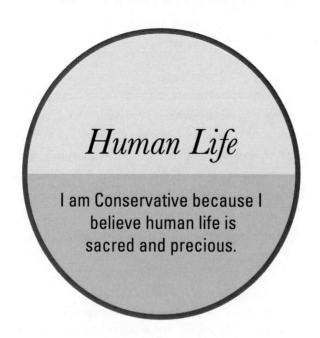

Human Life

I am Conservative because I believe human life is sacred and precious.

Innocent human life should be valued and protected from the moment a baby starts to grow from two tiny cells until the moment of natural death. Protecting the weakest and most helpless among us lifts the value of every human being. It gives healthy, strong citizens a chance to experience the joy that comes from being kind and caring for others who are less fortunate.

Nonconservatives believe it is acceptable for a mother to kill her baby before it is born, a procedure called abortion. They also believe it is okay for a doctor to kill an old or disabled person who doesn't want to live anymore or who needs expensive care, a practice called euthanasia. They want to allow scientists to experiment on preborn babies in the hope of finding cures for diseases, a method called embryonic stem-cell research. Embryonic stem cells come from a living, preborn baby who dies when its cells are used in this way. All of these processes have caused some people to stop valuing human life. As a result, many people are now very selfish, putting their own well-being and convenience ahead of everyone else's.

> If we accept that a mother can kill even her own child, how can we tell other people to not kill each other? Any country that accepts abortion is not teaching its people to love, but to use any violence to get what they want.
> —Mother Teresa of Calcutta

> Abortion is advocated only by persons who have themselves been born.
> —Ronald Reagan

> This day I call heaven and earth as witnesses against you that I have set before you life and death, blessings and curses. Now choose life, so that you and your children may live.
> —Deuteronomy 30:19

Dinner-Table Dialogue:

- When is it acceptable to cause death for one person in order to save another?

- When does human life begin?

Info Quest:

- Conservatives are usually in favor of more individual freedoms. How do Conservatives justify laws against abortion and euthanasia if someone wants to choose those for themselves?

- What cures have been discovered from embryonic stem cell research?

- What cures have been discovered from adult stem cell research?

Danger of Power

I am Conservative because
I believe people become
dangerous when they
are too powerful.

Power is addictive. Most people, when they get a taste of power, want more and more. A person of good character will guard themselves against this. Conservatives realize this about human nature. They are glad the Constitution limits the power of government and our elected representatives, even those they like and agree with.

Nonconservatives think the Constitution puts too many limits on government. They are willing to put much trust in the elected representatives they like and agree with. They don't seem to understand what power does to human nature. Nonconservatives think elected representatives are smarter and more capable than citizens, so they are willing to let elected representatives take control of decisions and seize as much power as they can.

> In questions of power, then, let no more be said of confidence in man, but bind him down from mischief by the chains of the Constitution.
> —Thomas Jefferson

> Experience hath shown that even under the best forms (of government) those entrusted with power have, in time, and by slow operations, perverted it into tyranny.
> —Thomas Jefferson

> The greater the power, the more dangerous the abuse.
> —Edmund Burke

> Constant experience shows us that every man invested with power is apt to abuse it and to carry authority as far as it will go.
> —Charles Montesquieu

It is the duty of the patriot to protect his country from his government.

—Thomas Paine

All men having power ought to be distrusted to a certain degree.

—James Madison

Because power corrupts, society's demands for moral authority and character increase as the importance of the position increases.

—John Adams

Dinner-Table Dialogue:

- How do elected representatives gain power?

- How can you tell if an elected representative is using their power to improve the country or if they are using their power for their own gain? Name some leaders through history who have abused their power. Name some who have done right with their power.

Limited Government

I am Conservative because I believe
in small, limited government.

Conservatives believe government should be small and limited. This means it should employ the fewest number of people, tax the lowest amount, and seek the minimum amount of power necessary to protect citizens' individual rights and freedoms. Conservatives also believe government should be local. This means city and state laws, rather than federal laws in general, should protect the interests of the citizens who live there.

The federal government has made many laws that go beyond the power given to it in the Constitution. This is called government over-reach. If there is nothing written in the Constitution about a particular issue, then each individual state is allowed to make its own law about that issue.

Nonconservatives prefer a large, powerful federal government that makes laws for states and every citizen. This usually isn't a good idea, because different areas of the United States have very different needs and problems. Most problems should be solved by the people nearest to the problem, who have direct knowledge of it. However, Nonconservatives want government to be responsible for numerous services and be located in one place (Washington, DC). They think elected representatives know what is best and should be given a lot of power over citizens' lives.

> I think we have more machinery of government than is necessary, too many parasites living on the labor of the industrious.
>
> —Thomas Jefferson

> If Congress can employ money indefinitely to the general welfare, and are the sole and supreme judges of the general welfare, they may take … in short, every thing, from the highest object of state legislation down to the most minute ob-

ject of police, would be thrown under the power of Congress...Were the power of Congress to be established in the latitude contended for, it would subvert the very foundations, and transmute the very nature of the limited government established by the people of America.

—James Madison

Dinner-Table Dialogue:

- Name some rules in your family that other families may not have. Should every family have the same rules? Why or why not? Should every city and state have to follow the same laws? Why or why not?

- If a city passes laws that citizens dislike, citizens can move to a different city. They can also move to a different state if they disagree with its laws, although that may be more difficult. What happens when the federal government passes disagreeable laws?

- Take another look at Thomas Jefferson's quote in this chapter. What did he mean when he compared government to parasites?

Government Provision

I am Conservative because I believe government should only provide what individuals can't accomplish on their own.

Conservatives don't expect government to assume their individual responsibilities. They think elected representatives should spend revenue (taxpayer money) only to serve and protect citizens in ways they cannot, individually. The federal government should not use tax revenue to pay for projects that benefit only the citizens of a particular state. Programs and services should be paid for by the taxpayer citizens who will benefit from them. For example, the federal government should provide military protection for its citizens. State and city governments should provide services like roads, a water system, prisons, and schools. However, some Conservatives believe private businesses could manage these services better than government does.

Nonconservatives want citizens to pay taxes and let the federal government decide how to spend the revenue. When this happens, citizens don't have enough input on how their tax money is spent. They pay taxes for far-away projects they do not need and will never use. Nonconservatives also like the idea of the government using revenue to provide for everyone's needs. Some sincerely believe that this is a good way to take care of needy people. However, when the government provides benefits, it can easily gain power over the lives of citizens by controlling their behavior. Also, it causes citizens to stop taking responsibility for their own lives.

> I predict future happiness for Americans if they can prevent the government from wasting the labors of the people under the pretense of taking care of them.
> —Thomas Jefferson

✸ ✸ ✸

I think the best way of doing good to the poor, is not making them easy in poverty, but leading or driving them out of it. In my youth I travelled much, and I observed in different countries, that the more public provisions were made for the poor, the less they provided for themselves, and of course became poorer. And, on the contrary, the less was done for them, the more they did for themselves, and became richer.

—Ben Franklin

The past shows unvaryingly that when a people's freedom disappears, it goes not with a bang, but in silence amid the comfort of being cared for. That is the dire peril in the present trend toward statism. If freedom is not found accompanied by a willingness to resist, and to reject favors, rather than to give up what is intangible but precarious, it will not long be found at all.

—Richard Weaver

Dinner-Table Dialogue:

- What are some tax-funded projects your family benefits from?

- What are some tax-funded projects your family will probably never get to use or even see?

Info Quest:

- What are "pork-barrel politics" or "earmarks"? Give some examples. What do you think of these practices?

Low Taxes

I am Conservative because I believe taxes should be as low as possible, and every citizen should share in paying them.

Federal, state, and city governments tax almost every activity of citizens' lives. Some taxes are necessary to provide what individual citizens cannot accomplish on their own. But when citizens are forced to pay high taxes, they don't have as much money to spend, invest, donate, or save.

Every citizen does receive some personal benefit from the taxes they pay. However, high taxes take away citizens' freedom, because their choice of how to spend their money is taken away, and their money ends up benefiting someone else instead of themselves or their family. Conservatives believe in freedom for all citizens, rich or poor. Citizens who earn a lot of money are often the ones who open businesses and spend money in the free market, creating jobs for others. Forcing them to pay high taxes cuts their ability to do these things.

Nonconservatives want to take from citizens that have earned more, and give to those that have earned less (this is called socialism). In the name of fairness, Nonconservatives say that the poorest people should not have to pay any taxes. They stir up jealousy against successful citizens. They believe government should be a powerful provider of people's needs, so they use tax revenue as a way to accomplish that goal.

As long as there is any kind of tax, all citizens should have to pay it. If everyone pays, everyone feels ownership in how the revenue is spent and has personal motivation to keep taxes low.

> Each individual of the society has a right to be protected by it in the enjoyment of his life, liberty, and property, according to standing laws. He is obliged, consequently, to contribute his share to the expense of this protection; and to give his personal service, or an equivalent,

when necessary. But no part of the property of any individual can, with justice, be taken from him, or applied to public uses, without his own consent, or that of the representative body of the people.

—John Adams

You cannot help the poor by destroying the rich. You cannot strengthen the weak by weakening the strong. You cannot bring about prosperity by discouraging thrift. You cannot lift the wage earner up by pulling the wage payer down. You cannot further the brotherhood of man by inciting class hatred. You cannot build character and courage by taking away people's initiative and independence. You cannot help people permanently by doing for them, what they could and should do for themselves.

—William Boetcker

Dinner-Table Dialogue:

- What is the sales tax rate where you live? Should everyone have to pay the same percentage? Would you like to pay more so someone else wouldn't have to pay any?

- What is your opinion of the progressive income tax?

- What is the fairest way to tax citizens?

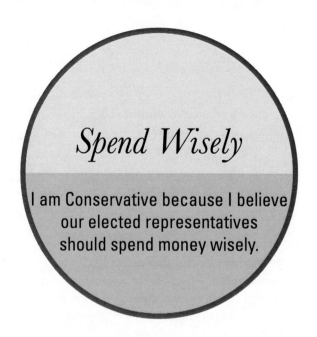

Spend Wisely

I am Conservative because I believe
our elected representatives
should spend money wisely.

This is called fiscal responsibility. A government's revenue comes from citizens who have worked and paid taxes. Elected representatives should keep a balanced budget (not spend more than they receive), just like citizens are expected to do in their homes. They should not run up debt that the next generation of taxpayers will have to pay. Doing so steals young citizens' freedom and their chance for a successful future.

Nonconservatives may agree with the idea of a balanced budget, but their policies oppose it. They continue to tax citizens heavily, but spend even more.

They put our nation into debt for services that cause people to depend on government. They spend money to fund projects that many citizens do not need.

> Think what you do when you run in debt; you give to another power over your liberty.
> —Benjamin Franklin

> But with respect to future debt; would it not be wise and just for that nation to declare in the constitution they are forming that neither the legislature, nor the nation itself can validly contract more debt, than they may pay within their own age, or within the term of 19 years.
> —Thomas Jefferson

> The wicked borrow and do not repay, but the righteous give generously.
> Psalm 37:21

> Do not be a man who strikes hands in pledge or puts up security for debts; if you lack the means to pay, your very bed will be snatched from under you.
> Proverbs 22:26–27

Dinner-Table Dialogue:

- What is your opinion of the national debt that was passed to you from previous voters and elected representatives?

- What benefits do you or your family receive that are paid for by current and future taxpayers?

- Does your family keep a balanced budget, or spend more than you earn? How much personal debt does your family owe for a home, car, or other items?

✷ ✷ ✷   61

Government Benefits

I am Conservative because I know government benefits are not "free."

Many citizens think government benefits are free, and mistakenly use the word "free" to describe them. Some examples are public schools and the programs they provide such as special education, meals, and counseling; public libraries; parks, trails, and playgrounds; benefits for the poor and elderly such as medical care, food, and housing; disaster relief and rebuilding. The list is endless, with some necessary things and many wasteful things. Conservatives realize these programs and services should never be called "free" because the money to pay for them comes from taxpayer citizens.

Nonconservatives are happy to call government programs and services "free." They want people to sign up for benefits that will make them depend on government. It seems they don't want people to realize that another citizen is paying for the benefits they are getting. This has created an enormous group of people who think it is all right to let other citizens or the government take care of them and their responsibilities.

There is no such thing as a free lunch.
—attributed to Paul Mallon

What one person receives without working for, another person must work for without receiving. The government cannot give to anybody anything that the government does not first take from somebody else.
— Adrian Rogers

Go to the ant, you sluggard; consider its ways and be wise! It has no commander, no overseer or ruler, yet it stores its provisions in summer and gathers its food at harvest.
Proverbs 6:6–8

Dinner-Table Dialogue:

- What are some government programs or services that you or others refer to as "free"? Take a few minutes to practice saying "tax-funded" instead.

- Think of a time when you received something that was provided at no cost to you. Who actually paid for it?

Helping and Donating

I am Conservative because I believe in helping others and donating to causes I believe in.

When hardship strikes our fellow citizens or people around the world, Americans want to help. When we believe in a worthy cause, we want to support it.

Conservatives believe that helping others works best when citizens can donate to whoever they want to, when they want to, because they want to. When citizens are taxed to help others or support causes, the revenue might be spent on something a citizen does not agree with. In addition, when citizens pay high taxes, they don't have as much money to donate.

Nonconservatives think elected representatives

know how to spend money better than the citizens who earned it. They want tax revenue to be spent on social programs that are supposed to help needy people. The problem is, the government system is not effective. Our representatives end up wasting some, losing some, using some to pay themselves, then sending a portion to wherever they decide it should be spent. After all this, less money goes to help the people who truly need it.

> I can find no warrant for such an appropriation in the Constitution, and I do not believe that the power and duty of the General Government ought to be extended to the relief of individual suffering which is in no manner properly related to the public service or benefit.
> —Grover Cleveland

> To compel a man to furnish funds for the propagation of ideas he disbelieves and abhors is sinful and tyrannical.
> —Thomas Jefferson

> Charity is no part of the legislative duty of the government.
> —James Madison

✷ ✷ ✷

I cannot undertake to lay my finger on that article of the Constitution which granted a right to Congress of expending, on objects of benevolence, the money of their constituents.

—James Madison

Each man should give what he has decided in his heart to give, not reluctantly or under compulsion, for God loves a cheerful giver.

2 Corinthians 9:7

For I was hungry and you gave me something to eat, I was thirsty and you gave me something to drink, I was a stranger and you invited me in, I needed clothes and you clothed me, I was sick and you looked after me, I was in prison and you came to visit me. Then the righteous will answer him, "Lord, when did we see you hungry and feed you, or thirsty and give you something to drink? When did we see you a stranger and invite you in, or needing clothes and clothe you? When did we see you sick or in prison and go to visit you?" The King will reply, "I tell you the truth, whatever you did for one of the least of these brothers of mine, you did for me."

Matthew 25:35–40

Dinner-Table Dialogue:

- When has your family donated to someone in need or to a cause you believe in?

- What are some social programs you would not support with your taxes if you had a choice?

✱ ✱ ✱

Capitalism

I am Conservative because
I believe in capitalism.

Capitalism is also called free enterprise or the free market. In a capitalist economy, citizens are free to start a business of their own. Businesses compete to offer the best product or service for the best quality and price. Citizens make their own decisions where to shop and what to buy. They are free to look for the best bargain. Capitalism also allows business owners to earn money and even get wealthy because of honest work and success. Conservatives believe businesses should succeed or fail without interference or aid from the government. They believe less government intrusion leads to a stronger economy and greater freedom.

Nonconservatives hinder the free market by adding taxes, fixing prices, and imposing rules and regulations. Sometimes they take over businesses and make the government the seller. Sometimes they create government-owned monopolies (a business with no competition) because they want government to be powerful. Government does not do a good job managing business because there is no direct ownership and no one really cares whether or not the business succeeds.

> I take it that it is best for all to leave each man free to acquire property as fast as he can. Some will get wealthy. I don't believe in a law to prevent a man from getting rich; it would do more harm than good.
>
> —Abraham Lincoln

> It is not from the benevolence of the butcher, the brewer, or the baker that we expect our dinner, but from their regard to their own interest.
>
> —Adam Smith

✹ ✹ ✹

Dinner-Table Dialogue:

- Do you know anyone who started a business of their own? What risks have they taken to be successful?

- How does capitalism allow citizens to save money and get what they want?

- Why does capitalism allow some businesses to succeed and others to fail? Is this fair?

- What are some problems with monopolies?

Socialism

I am Conservative because I
believe socialism is a corrupt
and disastrous system.

Conservatives realize the Constitution guarantees
equal rights, but not equal property. Citizens have equal
opportunity, but there is no guarantee of equal results.
Citizens who work hard and take risks sometimes make
money for their efforts. Conservatives believe citizens
have the right to keep what they earn, or spend it the
way they want to, rather than being forced to give it to
others who aren't taking risks and may not be working hard. If people work hard but don't get rewarded,
eventually they quit. After that happens, there aren't
enough workers to support those who won't work.

The dream behind socialism is that everyone ends up with an equal amount of money or property. Under socialism, individuals are expected to work, place their rewards for work (money, crops, goods) into a common stockpile, then take only what they need, whether it is less or more than what they contributed. While this may sound nice, Conservatives understand that socialism has proven to be a failing system. Socialists think people will work as much as they can, then take as little as possible. The reality is most people will work as little as they can, and take as much as possible. As a result, socialism actually punishes success and rewards irresponsibility. It is theft, because a citizen's money is his or her own private property.

> The first requisite of a good citizen in this republic of ours is that he shall be able and willing to pull his own weight.
> —Theodore Roosevelt

> The Utopian schemes of leveling [redistribution], and a community of goods, are as visionary and impracticable as those which vest all property in the Crown. [These ideas] are arbitrary, despotic, and in our government unconsti-

✻ ✻ ✻

tutional. Now, what property can the colonists be conceived to have, if their money may be granted away by others, without their consent?
—Samuel Adams

The inherent vice of capitalism is the unequal sharing of blessings; the inherent virtue of socialism is the equal sharing of miseries.

—Winston Churchill

The essence of socialism is the attenuation [decrease] and ultimate abolition [elimination] of private property rights. Attacks on private property include, but are not limited to, confiscating the rightful property of one person and giving it to another to whom it doesn't belong. When this is done privately, we call it theft. When it's done collectively, we use euphemisms: income transfers or redistribution... Reaching into one's own pocket to assist his fellow man is noble and worthy of praise. Reaching into another person's pocket to assist one's fellow man is despicable and worthy of condemnation.

—Walter Williams

Dinner-Table Dialogue:

When you earn money, who should decide what to do with that money?

Imagine a school project on which you spent a lot of time, did your best, and earned a high score. Your classmate threw a project together at the last minute and earned a low score. How would you feel if the teacher took some of your points and gave them to your classmate? Is this the same or different than the way socialism deals with money?

Info Quest:

Early American colonists attempted socialism at Jamestown Colony in 1607 and Plymouth Plantation in 1620. Find out what happened.

✻ ✻ ✻

Climate Change

I am Conservative because I do not believe in manmade climate change.

The earth's climate goes through cycles of cooling and warming that people do not control and cannot change. These include ocean temperatures and solar (sun) activity. All citizens should take care of our planet and the creatures upon it. However, we do not need to live in fear that we are destroying the earth by simply living, using energy and technology, or making improvements to our way of life. We should make decisions based on reason and good science, not emotions and ideology.

Nonconservatives say people and pollution are responsible for climate change. This has not been proven, and there is a lot of evidence against it. Nonconservatives want to use the environment as an excuse to make more laws, control people's behavior, and tax them more. Many environmentalists think that to protect the environment, we have to keep the earth's conditions exactly the same as they were at some point in the past. However, the earth naturally goes through periods of warming and cooling; it is constantly changing.

> Hundreds of research studies in recent decades have found a moderate, natural 1500-year climate cycle that explains the earth's pre-industrial 0.5 degree C warming from 1850 to 1940, and may also explain much of the very modest 0.2 degree C net warming since 1940. If increased atmospheric CO_2 has produced nothing more than 0.1 degree or so of warming in the last 65 years, we may need to rethink the whole global warming issue.
> —Dennis T. Avery

> [I]n the great scheme of trade-offs in the history of humanity, never has there been a better one than trading a tiny amount of global warming for a massive amount of global prosperity.
> —Jonah Goldberg

God blessed them and said to them, "Be fruit-ful and increase in number; fill the earth and subdue it. Rule over the fish of the sea and the birds of the air and over every living creature that moves on the ground."

Genesis 1:28

Dinner-Table Dialogue:

- Name some things you enjoy that are only possible because of electricity and fossil fuels.

- Do you believe man-made climate change is real?

- Do you believe natural cooling and warming cycles are real?

- Does your family "reduce, reuse, recycle"? Why or why not?

Info Quest:

- Greenland is mostly covered in ice, so why is it called Greenland?

- Who are some well-known people that give a lot of advice about "going green" or being a good environmentalist? What kind of cars or airplanes do they use? How big are their houses? Do they eat meat? Does their advice match their actions?

Energy

I am Conservative because I believe United States energy companies should be allowed to supply the energy our country needs.

This is called energy independence. Electric companies need to be able to get coal. Nuclear power plants should be built in more places. Oil companies need more places to drill. Buying oil from other countries is dangerous, because they could decide to stop selling it to us. That would make fuel costs, then all other costs, go up.

Energy companies should generate as little pollution as possible, and keep learning how to provide clean energy. However, environmental concerns should be balanced with our country's needs for energy. Citizens and companies should be encouraged to research and invent new energy ideas. Those ideas should succeed if the free market, not taxpayer money, can support them for the long term. Until we come up with something new that works, we need to let the old ideas meet our energy needs.

Conservatives believe people are the earth's most precious resource. Nonconservatives think government and the environment are more important than people and their needs. As a result, they restrict oil companies from drilling where there is lots of oil. They charge high taxes on gasoline. They think coal-powered electricity causes too much pollution. They think nuclear power plants are hazardous. They want to use taxpayers' money to subsidize (support) energies the free market cannot sustain.

> America must get to work producing more energy. [Our] program for solving economic problems is based on growth and productivity. Large amounts of oil and natural gas lay beneath our land and off our shores, untouched because the present administration seems to believe the American people would rather see more regulation, more taxes, and more controls than more energy.

Coal offers great potential. So does nuclear energy produced under rigorous safety standards. It could supply electricity for thousands of industries and millions of jobs and homes. It must not be thwarted by a tiny minority opposed to economic growth which often finds friendly ears in regulatory agencies for its obstructionist campaigns.

Now, make no mistake. We will not permit the safety of our people or our environmental heritage to be jeopardized, but we are going to reaffirm that the economic prosperity of our people is a fundamental part of our environment.

—Ronald Reagan

Dinner-Table Dialogue:

- Why does an increase in fuel costs lead to an increase in all other costs?

- The United States has been called "the Saudi Arabia of coal." What does this mean?

- Why is it important that the free market, not taxpayers, support energy solutions?

Info Quest:

- How long has it been since a nuclear power plant has been built in the United States? What about an oil refinery or an electrical power plant?

Immigrants

I am Conservative because I believe immigrants should come to the United States legally, know English, and be ready to work.

Every nation has laws regarding its borders and who is allowed to enter. The United States is no different, and Conservatives want these laws to be enforced. Immigrants should follow our rules and wait their turn to come to the United States. They should be ready to work legally and contribute to the economy, not just expect the benefits of citizenship.

More than half of the states in the US have adopted English as their official language. A common language helps unite a nation. In addition, it is enormously expensive to provide translations for all the information a non-English speaker needs.

Nonconservatives support amnesty (overlooking the crime) for immigrants who come to the United States illegally. They think tax revenue should be spent on education, medical care, and other services for illegal immigrants. They also say schools, hospitals, and government offices should use tax revenue to provide translations.

Dishonest employers hire illegal immigrants because they will work for low wages and save money for the employer. This decreases wages for legal American workers and also makes fewer jobs available for them.

> The bosom of America is open to receive not only the opulent and respectable stranger, but the oppressed and persecuted of all nations and religions; whom we shall welcome to a participation of all our rights and privileges, if by decency and propriety of conduct they appear to merit the enjoyment.
> —George Washington

✴ ✴ ✴

We can have no "50–50" allegiance in this country. Either a man is an American and nothing else, or he is not an American at all.

—Theodore Roosevelt

Citizens have a right to expect the government to enforce the laws regarding who may cross our borders. Border security is a question of national sovereignty, national security and the government fulfilling its divinely mandated responsibility to enforce the law.

—Richard Land

The community is to have the same rules for you and for the alien living among you; this is a lasting ordinance for the generations to come. You and the alien shall be the same before the Lord.

Numbers 15:15

Everyone must submit himself to the governing authorities, for there is no authority except that which God has established. The authorities that exist have been established by God.

Romans 13:1

Dinner-Table Dialogue:

- It is against the law to hire people who cannot legally work due to age or citizenship. What is your opinion of this?

- What are some consequences of illegal immigration in our country?

- How should you treat someone who can't speak English?

Info Quest:

- Has your state adopted English as its official language? What areas does this affect? What difference does it make?

Government Protection

I am Conservative because I believe the United States government should protect its citizens against enemies.

This is called a strong national defense. It is expensive, but the United States needs proper equipment, technology, and a well-trained military that is always ready to protect its citizens when enemies near or far try to harm us.

Nonconservatives think if we talk nicely to our enemies, they will see things our way and become our friends. Or, if we let our enemies have what they want, they will leave us alone. Because of different cultures and beliefs all over the world, this approach simply does not work.

There is a rank due to the United States among nations which will be withheld, if not absolutely lost, by the reputation of weakness. If we desire to avoid insult, we must be able to repel it; if we desire to secure peace, one of the most powerful instruments of our rising prosperity, it must be known that we are at all times ready for war.

—George Washington

War is an ugly thing, but not the ugliest of things. The decayed and degraded state of moral and patriotic feeling which thinks that nothing is worth war is much worse. The person who has nothing for which he is willing to fight, nothing which is more important than his own personal safety, is a miserable creature and has no chance of being free unless made and kept so by the exertions of better men than himself.

—John Stuart Mill

To insist on strength is not war-mongering. It is peace-mongering.

—Barry Goldwater

✷ ✷ ✷

We sleep soundly in our beds because rough men stand ready in the night to visit violence on those who would do us harm.

—attributed to George Orwell
and Winston Churchill

Dinner-Table Dialogue:

- Who do bullies bother: strong kids who fight back, or weak kids who beg for mercy and give up their lunch money?

- Is defending our country's citizens and our way of life worrh the high price?

Info Quest:

- What is the federal budget for defense? How does it compare to social programs and the treasury department?

Self Protection

I am Conservative because I believe citizens have the right to protect themselves.

Citizens can usually depend on the police or other good people to help protect them from harm. When help can't come quickly enough, citizens should be allowed protect themselves and their families against anyone who is threatening their safety. Most of the time people defend themselves without using a gun, but sometimes guns or other weapons are needed.

Nonconservatives make laws that take away citizens' rights to own guns. However, criminals will not obey these laws, so they will have guns but law-abiding citizens will not have an equal way to protect themselves. Nonconservatives think more laws will make citizens safer. However, history has shown that disarming citizens does not benefit them, it makes them defenseless and easier to abuse. Nonconservative elected officials want people to depend on them for protection, which increases their power.

> Laws that forbid the carrying of arms ... disarm only those who are neither inclined nor determined to commit crimes ... Such laws make things worse for the assaulted and better for the assailants; they serve rather to encourage than to prevent homicides, for an unarmed man may be attacked with greater confidence than an armed man.
>
> —Thomas Jefferson

> Americans have the right and advantage of being armed—unlike the citizens of other countries whose governments are afraid to trust the people with arms.
>
> —James Madison

> The Constitution shall never be construed ... to prevent the people of the United States who are peaceable citizens from keeping their own arms.
>
> —Samuel Adams

✸ ✸ ✸

Dinner-Table Dialogue:

- Do you have guns or other weapons in your home? Why or why not?

- What kind of victim do criminals prefer: those who can defend themselves, or those who cannot?

Info Quest:

- How do gun control laws affect crime rates?

✱ ✱ ✱

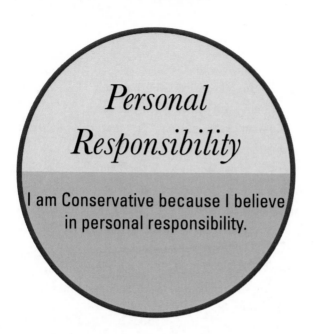

Personal Responsibility

I am Conservative because I believe in personal responsibility.

Conservatives believe each citizen can achieve his or her potential through hard work and effort. The United States is known around the world as the land of opportunity and freedom, and its citizens have many rights and privileges. In order to keep them, citizens must practice personal responsibility, such as: I get to choose the direction for my life. I am responsible for my choices, actions, feelings, thoughts, and how all these affect my life. I will not blame others for my choices or what I become. I will forgive others for hurting me and not see myself as a victim. I will not depend on others for something I can accomplish myself. However, I will accept help from others when I truly need it.

Nonconservatives may say that they believe in personal responsibility. However, they think it is acceptable for people to depend on government for their needs. Dependence causes people to lose confidence in their ability to provide for themselves. Nonconservatives allow people to think of themselves as victims, or that someone else should take care of them. This keeps people in a trap of feeling unable or unwilling to take care of themselves, and they depend on government as a result.

> Dependence begets subservience and venality, suffocates the germ of virtue, and prepares fit tools for the designs of ambition. [Dependence creates a lower class, causes corruption, suffocates the seed of virtue, and prepares one's thoughts for ideas of gain at any cost.]
>
> —Thomas Jefferson

> For you yourselves know how you ought to follow our example. We were not idle when we were with you, nor did we eat anyone's food without paying for it. On the contrary,

we worked night and day, laboring and toiling so that we would not be a burden to any of you. We did this, not because we do not have the right to such help, but in order to make ourselves a model for you to follow. For even when we were with you, we gave you this rule: "If a man will not work, he shall not eat." We hear that some among you are idle. They are not busy; they are busybodies. Such people we command and urge in the Lord Jesus Christ to settle down and earn the bread they eat.

2 Thessalonians 3:7–12

Dinner-Table Dialogue:

- Take another look at the "I" sentences in the first paragraph of this chapter. Which ones are you good at? Which ones leave room for improvement?

✻ ✻ ✻

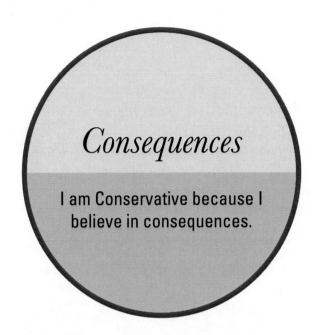

Consequences

I am Conservative because I
believe in consequences.

From the very beginning, the United States was
founded on the ideas of individual freedom and individual responsibility. As Americans, we are free to live
our lives in almost any way we choose. On the other
hand, we must take responsibility for our choices
and the consequences of our choices. Conservatives
understand this. They will take credit for their good
choices, and accept the results of their poor choices
without expecting other citizens to pay for their mistakes. This includes making moral and healthy choices
or not, getting an education or not, buying insurance

or not, going into debt or not, saving money for old age or not, where they choose to live, and every decision they will ever make.

Nonconservatives allow people to avoid the negative results of poor decisions. They use tax revenue to aid people who are in trouble because of their own unwise choices. This enables people to keep making poor decisions because they don't feel any inconvenience from them. It rewards irresponsible behavior, increases a citizen's dependence on government, and decreases their initiative (reason to do something).

A compassionate person is willing to help others, even those who are in trouble because of their own bad choices. Conservatives want to help through voluntary donations, not taxes. In this way, they can directly help the person and influence them to make better choices in the future.

> If you could kick the person in the pants responsible for most of your trouble, you wouldn't sit for a month.
> —Theodore Roosevelt

In the long run, we shape our lives, and we shape ourselves. The process never ends until we die. And the choices we make are ultimately our responsibility.

—Eleanor Roosevelt

One of the annoying things about believing in free will and individual responsibility is the difficulty of finding somebody to blame your problems on. And when you do find somebody, it's remarkable how often his picture turns up on your driver's license.

—PJ O'Rourke

Can a man scoop fire into his lap without his clothes being burned?

Proverbs 6:27

Do not be deceived: God cannot be mocked. A man reaps what he sows.

Galatians 6:7–8

Dinner-Table Dialogue:

- What should a person do if they spend money on fun activities then run out of money for food or other needs? What should you do if you know someone like this?

- How does your family feel about paying higher insurance rates because of people who won't buy insurance?

- Not including paying taxes, what can you do to help someone who is in a difficult situation?

- Take another look at the list of choices in the first paragraph of this chapter. Which ones have you taken responsibility for? Which ones leave room for improvement?

You

I am Conservative because
I believe in you!

If you live in the United States, you already have a vast advantage over most everyone else in the world. You have education opportunities, clean water, abundant food, access to the best medical care, and many freedoms. You have riches that countless people can only imagine. Be worthy of this honor. Earn it. Do something tremendous with your life!

> The position of the Americans is therefore quite exceptional, and it may be believed that

no democratic people will ever be placed in a similar one.

                                    –Alexis de Tocqueville

The Americans took but little when they emigrated except what they stood up in and what they had in their souls. They came through, they tamed the wilderness, they became a refuge for the oppressed from every land and clime.

                                    –Winston Churchill

It has been my observation that most people get ahead during the time that others waste.

                                    –Henry Ford

Regardless of who you are or what you have been, you can be what you want to be.

                                    –W. Clement Stone

From everyone who has been given much, much will be demanded; and from the one who has been entrusted with much, much more will be asked.

                                    –Luke 12:48

✳ ✳ ✳

Dinner-Table Dialogue:

- What are some things you did today in the United States that many other people around the world are unable to do?

- What did you do to prepare for your future today?

- What did you do to learn and improve your mind today? Was it your best effort?

- What did you do to help someone today?

✸ ✸ ✸   111

Afterword

by Doug Hoffman

More than 230 years ago, our country's Founding Fathers took a stand against British oppression due to high taxes and other offenses against the freedoms of the Colonists resulting in the Declaration of Independence, the American Revolution and The Constitution of the United States.

All of these were implemented with deep thought, forward vision and intuition by the people and for the people forming the foundation of a Republic that would last through the test of time and change. Since then many Americans have given their lives to ensure these freedoms, ideals, and values.

In our modern society, many of the freedoms fixed by the Constitution are taken for granted and not fully appreciated.

Unfortunately for Thomas Paine, his "Common Sense" isn't too common any more, at least in Washington. Too many of those in government are career politicians who have never worked in either the private sector or run a business in the free enterprise system.

Career politicians were never envisioned by our Founders, yet they exist today and are imposing new laws, regulations and taxes that continually erode our personal freedoms, stifle the free enterprise system and kill jobs in America.

This has resulted in an America similar to our country's situation in 1776 in which the government doesn't work for the people but the people work for the government. A government that provides for all of our needs and controls every aspect of our lives is a government that can take away our independence and freedoms.

We must all remember that freedom is not free. I finally reached a point in my life where I could no longer sit idly by and watch our leaders and govern-

✹ ✹ ✹

ment spend money we don't have thereby creating deficits that can never be repaid by us, our children or our grandchildren; over regulate our citizens and businesses, and over tax us.

I never had a desire to become a politician and as a matter of fact had a general disdain for those who tell the voters what they want to hear during the election, but when sworn in to legislative office, vote as if they've never made those pledges to the voters. Thus, I decided that I had to run for the United States Congress in New York's 23rd Congressional District's Special Election in 2009.

Hopefully my candidacy awakened the silent majority who believe in these principles, values and ideals and we will continue this ideological revolution to retake America.

Melanie Angell Elliott's book *Why Am I Conservative* will help parents teach the basic conservative ideals of our Constitution and representative government to the next generation of American citizens, our children and grandchildren. These conservative ideals and values need to be once again emphasized in our society or educational institutions today.

You too can step forward and join this peaceful

revolution and help America by passing on the principles of conservatism as defined in this book to the children of America.

George Washington said it best: "A primary objective ... should be the education of our youth in the science of government. In a republic, what species of knowledge can be equally important? And what duty more pressing ... than communicating it to those who are to be the future guardians of the liberties of the country."

God bless America!

—Doug Hoffman
2009 Conservative US Congressional
Candidate, New York State 23rd
Congressional District Special Election

Follow Melanie Angell Elliott on Facebook or her website.

Facebook: Melanie Angell Elliott, Author

Website: MelanieAngellElliott.com